STEVEN SPIELBERG

Director and Producer of the Jurassic Park Series

Rebecca Felix

Checkerboard
Library

An Imprint of Abdo Publishing
abdopublishing.com

ABDOPUBLISHING.COM

Published by Abdo Publishing, a division of ABDO, PO Box 398166, Minneapolis, Minnesota 55439. Copyright © 2017 by Abdo Consulting Group, Inc. International copyrights reserved in all countries. No part of this book may be reproduced in any form without written permission from the publisher. Checkerboard Library™ is a trademark and logo of Abdo Publishing.

Printed in the United States of America, North Mankato, Minnesota

062016
092016

THIS BOOK CONTAINS
RECYCLED MATERIALS

Design: Christa Schneider, Mighty Media, Inc.
Production: Mighty Media, Inc.
Editor: Paige Polinsky
Cover Photograph: Shutterstock
Interior Photographs: Alamy, p. 5; AP Images, pp. 13, 22, 27, 28; Everett Collection NYC, pp. 7, 17, 19, 25; Getty Images, pp. 15, 21, 28; Shutterstock, pp. 9, 28; Yearbook Library, p. 11

Publishers Cataloging-in-Publication Data

Names: Felix, Rebecca, author.
Title: Steven Spielberg : director and producer of the Jurassic Park series / by Rebecca Felix.
Description: Minneapolis, MN : Abdo Publishing, [2017] | Series: Movie makers | Includes index.
Identifiers: LCCN 2016934271 | ISBN 9781680781861 (lib. bdg.) | ISBN 9781680775716 (ebook)
Subjects: LCSH: Spielberg, Steven, 1946- --Juvenile literature. | Motion picture producers and directors--United States--Biography--Juvenile literature. | Screenwriters--United States--Biography--Juvenile literature.
Classification: DDC 791.4302/33/092 [B]--dc23
LC record available at http://lccn.loc.gov/2016934271

CONTENTS

HOLLYWOOD LEGEND

The gleaming eye of a *Tyrannosaurus rex* fills the window of a car holding two children. A lost alien and a young boy become as close as brothers. And an **archaeologist** travels the world on wild adventures.

What do dinosaurs, aliens, and archaeologists have in common? Each appear in a Steven Spielberg hit movie! Spielberg is considered one of the most influential people in the history of filmmaking. He has worked on more than 100 films, mainly as a **director** or **producer**. These films include **blockbusters** such as *Jurassic Park*, *Jaws*, the Indiana Jones series, and more.

Spielberg has won more than 160 awards for his storytelling, leadership, and talent. In fact, he is thought to be the creator of the Hollywood blockbuster. His focus on human interactions

Director Steven Spielberg poses with a model dinosaur from his film *The Lost World: Jurassic Park*. Spielberg's movies feature major visual effects.

and relationships has greatly influenced modern filmmaking. This important moviemaker's **passion** for films began in his childhood. It all started with one trip to a movie theater.

CHAPTER 2

CIRCUS SURPRISE

Steven Allan Spielberg was born December 18, 1946, in Cincinnati, Ohio. He was Arnold Spielberg and Leah Adler's first child. Steven had three younger sisters. Their names were Anne, Sue, and Nancy.

Steven's mother was a piano player. His father was an **electrical engineer**. Arnold's job often required the Spielbergs to move. After leaving Ohio, the family lived in Haddonfield, New Jersey. They then moved to Phoenix, Arizona.

When Steven was about seven years old, he received some exciting news. His father was taking him to see a circus! The following weekend, Arnold drove Steven to the event. Steven prepared to see the amazing circus acts his father told him about. But he got a surprise.

A major train wreck takes place in *The Greatest Show on Earth*. Years later, Spielberg filmed his own version of the scene with some model trains.

Arnold had not taken Steven to a circus. They were at a theater, watching a circus movie. Steven had never seen a film before. The movie, 1952's *The Greatest Show on Earth*, amazed him. From that day on, Steven wanted to become a filmmaker.

MAKING MOVIES

Steven's love of movies grew throughout his childhood. At ten years old, Steven began filming his family's special occasions and events. He used his father's **super 8mm** film camera.

Steven also began writing and **shooting** short movies with **plots**. One movie earned Steven his photography badge in Boy Scouts. Steven also made horror films. And by 16 years old, Steven had created his first full-length film.

Firelight is a science-fiction film about aliens in spaceships attacking a town. Steven wrote, edited, and **directed** the film. He wrote its music too. Steven's school band performed the **score**.

The Spielberg family lived in Phoenix's Arcadia neighborhood for seven years. Steven later described the area as his "true boyhood home."

While making *Firelight*, Steven turned to his parents for support. Leah and Arnold allowed Steven to film **scenes** in their home. They even let him explode cherry pie filling in their kitchen! Leah often made snacks for her son's **cast** and crew.

Steven's family, friends, and school helped him accomplish his goal. Steven finished *Firelight* near the end of his second year of high school. The film had taken about six months to **shoot**. *Firelight* was released on March 24, 1964. It was screened at the Phoenix Little Theatre, a local movie theater.

The Spielbergs moved to Saratoga, California, the day after *Firelight*'s release. There, Steven finished high school. He also moved one step closer to his future in Hollywood.

CLOSE ENCOUNTERS

Firelight inspired Spielberg's future film, *Close Encounters of the Third Kind*. The 1977 alien movie was a major success. It was nominated for four Golden Globe Awards, including Best Motion Picture–Drama.

In Saratoga, Steven (*back row, second from left*) wrote for his high school newspaper, *The Falcon*. He wrote about school sporting events.

UNIVERSAL STUDIOS

Spielberg graduated high school in 1965. The summer after graduating, Spielberg visited family friends in Los Angeles, California. There, he joined a group tour of the Universal Studios lot. This was where the studio filmed its movies.

According to Spielberg, he snuck away from the tour and explored for hours. The next day, he returned to the lot. This time, he wore a suit and carried a briefcase. Spielberg pretended he worked for the studio. He made it past the guards and got busy meeting filmmakers!

Later interviews revealed that this story might not be completely true. Spielberg did tour the lot, but it might have been during high school. And while he did work there for a summer, the position was probably planned.

The Universal Studios lot in Los Angeles, California.
Spielberg says he took over an abandoned office while there.

Whichever story is correct, Spielberg was able to work alongside the studio's filmmakers. He met many different **directors** and **producers**. Spielberg's time at Universal Studios taught him a lot about the film and television industry. He saw firsthand how the professional filming process came together on **set**.

Spielberg wanted to study filmmaking in college. But his school, California State University, Long Beach, did not offer **cinematography**. So, Spielberg majored in English. He continued to make films on the weekends.

During this time, Spielberg created *Amblin'*, a short film about **hitchhikers**. Spielberg showed *Amblin'* to movie editor Chuck Silvers. Silvers had met Spielberg years earlier at Universal Studios. Silvers enjoyed the film and showed it to executives at Universal Studios. The executives wanted to buy and release *Amblin'*, but the offer they made was too low. *Amblin'* was released in 1968 by a different company.

Spielberg dropped out of college to focus on filmmaking. In 1969, Universal Studios offered Spielberg a job! He became a **director** for Universal Studio's television department. Over the next seven years, Spielberg would begin building his reputation as a great filmmaker.

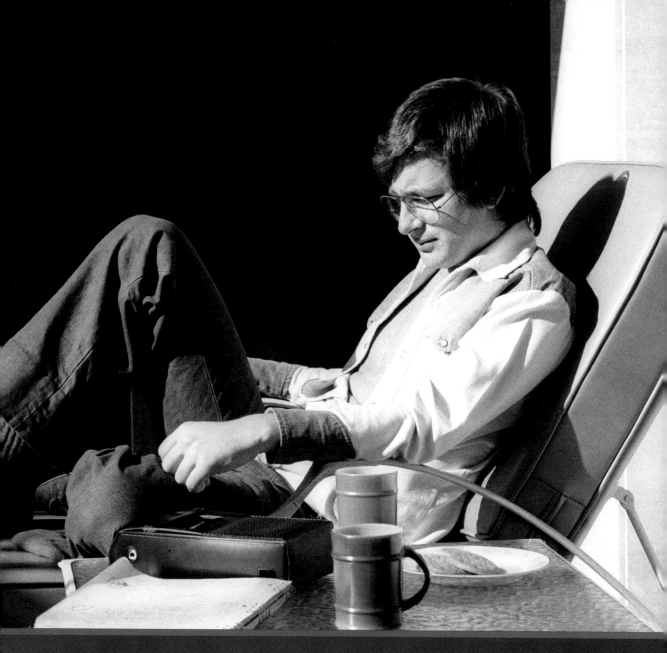

At 21 years old, Spielberg was one of the youngest directors ever hired by Universal Studios.

THRILLING
SUCCESS

Spielberg **directed** several television **episodes** for Universal Studios. In 1971, he directed a full-length movie. The film, *Duel*, originally **premiered** on television. Universal Studios then decided to make *Duel* a bit longer and release it in theaters overseas. The film's success allowed Spielberg to make more films for the studio.

Spielberg directed the action film *The Sugarland Express*, which released in 1974. The next year, Spielberg directed another film. It was the classic **thriller** *Jaws*.

HOT WATER

Jaws was a difficult movie to make. Bad weather delayed filming, and the robotic shark often stopped working. Production went over schedule by more than 100 days. Spielberg felt sure his career was over!

Spielberg and Bruce, the fake shark used in the film

Jaws is the story of a great white shark. The huge shark hunts swimmers along the coast of a resort town. The film was released in June 1975. It became a major hit.

Spielberg's shark **thriller** made more than $100 million in ticket sales. It was the first film in the United States to do so. It also won three **Academy Awards**, or Oscars. And several **critics** named the film one of the best movies of all time. The movie's success instantly made Spielberg a recognized Hollywood **director**.

ALIENS AND ADVENTURE

*J*aws began a wave of success for Spielberg. In 1977, he **directed** *Close Encounters of the Third Kind*. The science-fiction film earned Spielberg his first **Oscar** nomination for Best Director.

Spielberg soon started a new project with director George Lucas. Spielberg directed an adventure film based on Lucas's story. *Raiders of the Lost Ark* follows Indiana Jones, a heroic **archaeologist**. The 1981 film began a wildly successful series.

The next year, Spielberg's *E.T. the Extraterrestrial* hit theaters. Many **critics** called the alien film "an instant classic." Others said it made Spielberg one of the period's most popular filmmakers.

Spielberg decided to try **producing** films. In 1984, he cofounded production company Amblin Entertainment. The company produced several hits in the following years.

Spielberg poses with an E.T. puppet. Effects artist Carlo Rambaldi spent months designing the friendly alien's look.

FILM AND FAMILY

Spielberg and Lucas became great friends while working together. Lucas introduced Spielberg to actor Amy Irving. She and Spielberg married in 1985. They had a son, Max, later that year.

In 1989, Irving and Spielberg divorced. Spielberg began dating actor Kate Capshaw. Capshaw already had two children. She and Spielberg had a daughter, Sasha, in 1990. Spielberg and Capshaw married in 1991 and had a son, Sawyer, the next year.

THE COLOR PURPLE

Spielberg directed 1985's *The Color Purple,* based on the book by Alice Walker. The movie follows an African-American woman who overcomes a life of abuse. It was nominated for 11 Oscars.

Spielberg and Capshaw first met while filming *Indiana Jones and the Temple of Doom*. Capshaw played a lead role in the movie.

Life didn't slow down for Spielberg. *Jurassic Park*, **directed** by Spielberg, was released in 1993. It is the action-packed story of dinosaurs brought to life. Spielberg was praised for its thrilling **scenes**. He also became known for his busy schedule. Six months after *Jurassic Park*'s release, *Schindler's List* entered theaters. Spielberg directed this serious film about **World War II**.

Schindler's List earned Spielberg Academy Awards for Best Picture and Best Director in 1994.

Schindler's List brought Spielberg much success. The film won 75 awards, including seven **Oscars**. It also earned Spielberg his first Academy Award for Best **Director** in 1994.

Later that year, Spielberg cofounded a production company. He started Dreamworks SKG with **producers** Jeffrey Katzenberg and David Geffen. Spielberg worked as a lead producer for several projects. These included family films such as 1994's *The Flintstones* and 1995's *Casper*.

Meanwhile, Spielberg and Capshaw's large family grew even larger. In 1996, the couple adopted daughter Mikaela. That same year, Capshaw gave birth to another daughter, Destry.

CRITICS REACT

"... *Jurassic Park* lacks the emotional unity of Spielberg's classics (*Jaws*, *Close Encounters*, *E.T.*), yet it has enough of his innocent, playful **virtuosity** to send you out of the theater grinning with delight.... Spielberg is so good at setting up the wonders to come that he leaves us just about dizzy with **anticipation**."

—Owen Gleiberman,
Entertainment Weekly

"**The human characters are a ragtag bunch of half-realized, sketched-in personalities.** ... *Jurassic Park* throws a lot of dinosaurs at us, and because **they look terrific (and indeed they do), we're supposed to be grateful.** ... On the monster movie level, the movie works and is entertaining. But ... it could have been so much more."

—Roger Ebert,
Chicago Sun-Times

Both writers have good and bad things to say about Spielberg's work on *Jurassic Park*. In what ways are their opinions similar? How are they different?

ON THE SET OF
JURASSIC PARK

*J*urassic Park's original dinosaurs were mechanical models. Their movements were sped up with **special effects**. But Spielberg was disappointed with the result. He gathered a team of visual effects experts to work on other options.

This decision meant redoing months of work. But it also led to new special effects that would influence the future of **cinema**. Spielberg's team began developing **computer-generated imagery (CGI)** dinosaurs. CGI had been used in films before. But *Jurassic Park* would be one of the first movies to feature truly realistic CGI creatures.

Using CGI meant that the actors had to react to dinosaurs that weren't physically on **set**.

FAST FACT

Sound designers altered the sounds of whales, horses, geese, and other animals to create the dinosaur noises.

Spielberg works on a scene with actors Jeff Goldblum (*left*) and Laura Dern (*right*).

Special effects supervisor Dennis Muren (*right*) works with two members of his team.

However, Spielberg still used mechanical dinosaurs for some **scenes**. One featured a 17,500-pound *T. rex* attacking a car full of passengers. The actors didn't have to use their imagination for that scene!

Upon *Jurassic Park*'s release, viewers didn't have to use their imaginations either. The film's **special effects** were unlike anything anyone had ever seen. Spielberg's dinosaurs inspired other filmmakers to use **CGI** in their own works. The future of film was forever changed.

CHAPTER 8

CINEMA KING

While children kept Spielberg busy at home, dinosaurs kept him busy at work! Spielberg **directed** 1997's *The Lost World*, the **sequel** to *Jurassic Park*. He also directed *Saving Private Ryan*, which opened in 1998. It was praised for its realistic battle **scenes**.

In 2000, Spielberg was awarded the Director's Guild of America Lifetime Achievement Award. And in the following years, Spielberg worked on more than 60 projects. Most recently, he **produced** 2015's *Jurassic World*. It has been announced that Spielberg will also produce a fifth Jurassic Park film.

Today, Spielberg lives in Los Angeles, California. He loves watching **blockbusters** at the movie theater. Making hit films is still a part of Spielberg's daily life too. Whether directing aliens or crafting dinosaurs, Spielberg continues to make movie history.

In 2013, Spielberg served as the lead judge of the Cannes Film Festival in Paris, France. Cannes is one of the world's most recognized film festivals.

TIMELINE

1946
Steven Allan Spielberg is born December 18, in Cincinnati, Ohio.

1964
Spielberg's first full-length film, *Firelight*, is released on March 24.

1969
Universal Studios hires Spielberg as a director.

1975
Jaws is released. It is Spielberg's first big box-office hit.

1985
Spielberg marries Amy Irving. Their son Max is born later that year.

1989–1990
Spielberg and Irving divorce. Spielberg and Kate Capshaw have a daughter, Sasha, together.

FAMOUS WORKS

Jaws
Released 1975

More than 67 million people saw *Jaws* in theaters.

Won: Outstanding Film of 1975, Academy of Science Fiction, Fantasy & Horror Films, 1976

Raiders of the Lost Ark
Released 1981

Indiana Jones was named after George Lucas's dog, Indiana.

Nominated: Best Director, Academy Awards, 1982

E.T. the Extraterrestrial
Released 1982

Spielberg shot *E.T.* at a lower height, as if from a child's view.

Won: Best Motion Picture–Drama, Golden Globe Awards, 1985

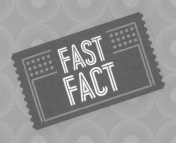
Spielberg used all of his *Schindler's List* profits to open The Righteous Persons Foundation. It supports Jewish communities around the United States.

1991
Spielberg and Capshaw marry.

1992
Spielberg and Capshaw's son, Sawyer, is born.

1994
Spielberg cofounds production company Dreamworks SKG.

1996
Spielberg and Capshaw adopt daughter Mikaela. Their daughter Destry is born later that year.

2000
Spielberg wins the Director's Guild of America Lifetime Achievement Award.

2015
Jurassic World, produced by Spielberg, is released.

Indiana Jones and the Temple of Doom
Released 1984

In one scene, actor Kate Capshaw was covered in bugs.

Won: Best Visual Effects, Academy Awards, 1985

Jurassic Park
Released 1993

All together, dinosaurs only appear in about 15 minutes of this film!

Won: Favorite Motion Picture, People's Choice Awards, 1994

Jurassic World
Released 2015

This film is the third-highest earning movie in history.

Won: Visual Effects of the Year, Hollywood Film Awards, 2015

GLOSSARY

Academy Award – one of several awards the Academy of Motion Picture Arts and Sciences gives to the best actors and filmmakers of the year.

anticipation – a feeling of excitement about something that is going to happen.

archaeologist (ahr-kee-AH-luh-jihst) – one who studies the remains of people and activities from ancient times.

blockbuster – something that is very large, expensive, or successful.

cast – the actors in a play, movie, or television program.

cinema – the movie industry. *Cinematography* is the art and science of photographing motion pictures.

computer-generated imagery (CGI) – images created on a computer and used for visual effects in films and TV shows.

confidence – the state or feeling of being certain.

critic – a professional who gives his or her opinion on art, literature, or performances.

direct – to supervise people in a play, movie, or television program. Someone who directs is a *director*.

electrical engineer – someone who is trained to design electrical systems used in communications and machinery.

episode – one of the programs in a television or movie series.

Golden Globe Award – an award recognizing excellence in both the movie and television industries.

hitchhiker – a traveler who gets free rides from drivers passing by.

Oscar – see *Academy Award*.

WEBSITES

To learn more about Movie Makers, visit booklinks.abdopublishing.com. These links are routinely monitored and updated to provide the most current information available.

passion – great devotion or enthusiasm.

plot – the main story of a novel, movie, play, or any work of fiction.

premiere – to have a first performance or exhibition.

produce – to oversee staff and funding to put on a play or make a movie or TV show. Someone who produces is a *producer*.

ragtag – made up of different things and not organized or put together well.

scene – a part of a play, movie, or TV show that presents what is happening in one particular place and time.

score – music written to accompany a play or a movie.

sequel (SEE-kwuhl) – a book, movie, or other work that continues the story begun in a preceding one.

set – an artificial setting where a play is performed or a movie or television program is filmed.

shoot – to film a movie or video.

special effects – visual or sound effects used in a movie or television program.

super 8mm – a film format used in a type of home movie camera.

thriller – an exciting story that is filled with action, mystery, or suspense.

virtuosity – great ability or skill.

World War II – from 1939 to 1945, fought in Europe, Asia, and Africa. Great Britain, France, the United States, the Soviet Union, and their allies were on one side. Germany, Italy, Japan, and their allies were on the other side.

INDEX